What's in this book

学习内容 Contents   2

读一读 Read   4

听听说说 Listen and say   12

写一写 Write   16

多元学习 Connections   18

温习 Checkpoint   20

分享 Sharing   22

This book belongs to

_____

你喜欢什么活动?
What activities do you like?

学习内容 Contents

沟通 Communication

说说活动喜好
Talk about activities that one likes

背景介绍：
吴老师在课堂上跟学生们讨论
大家喜欢的休闲活动。

生词 New words

★	玩	to play
★	活动	activity
★	电视	television
★	踢	to kick
★	足球	football
★	打球	to play ball games
★	还是	or
	玩具	toy
	电脑	computer
	高兴	happy

你喜欢玩玩具，还是喜欢看电视？
Do you like playing with toys or watching television?

你喜欢吃饼干，还是喜欢做饼干呢？
Do you like eating biscuits or making them?

跨学科学习 Project

调查活动喜好，并完成活动金字塔
Do a survey on activities and finish
the activity pyramid

文化 Cultures

中国传统活动
Traditional Chinese activities

参考答案：
1 I like to read books./I like to play basketball.
2 I prefer individual activities/group activities.
3 My favourite activity is drawing/playing computer games.

Get ready

1 What do you like to do in your spare time?

2 Do you prefer individual or group activities?

3 What is your favourite activity?

故事大意：
伊森和好朋友们都有各自喜爱的休闲活动。

提醒学生，这个故事是
以伊森的视角叙述的。

huó dòng
活动

放学回家后，你喜欢做
什么活动？

参考问题和答案：

1 Which activity in the picture do you like? (I like playing ten
playing with toys.)

2 What do you like to do when you get home after school?
(I like playing with my dog/watching TV.)

kàn diàn shì

看电视

hái shì

还是

"还是"表示选择，当句子中有两个或以上的选项时，可以将"还是"放在最后一个选项前。

wán wán jù

玩玩具

你喜欢玩玩具，还是看电视？

参考问题和答案：

1　What is Elsa doing? (She is watching TV.)

2　Do you prefer watching TV or playing with toys? (I prefer watching TV/ playing with toys.)

tī
踢

zú qiú
足球

dǎ qiú
打球

你喜欢踢足球吗？喜欢
打球吗？

参考问题和答案：

1 What is Hao Hao doing? (He is playing football.)
2 What is Ivan doing? (He is playing tennis.)
3 Do you like playing football or tennis? (I like playing football./
  I do not like either of them.)

wán diàn nǎo
玩电脑

很多人喜欢玩电脑，你觉得怎么样？

参考问题和答案：

1 What is Ling Ling doing? (She is playing on the computer.)

2 Do you like playing on the computer? (Yes, it is fun./No, it is bad for my eyes.)

7

gāo xìng

高兴

参考问题和答案:

1 What is Ethan doing? (He is making biscuits.)

2 Do you think he likes making biscuits? Why? (Yes, because he looks happy.)

3 What is Ethan going to do with the biscuits he makes? (He is going to share them with his friends.)

我喜欢做饼干。和大家一起分享,我很高兴。

你喜欢吃饼干，还是做饼干呢？

参考问题和答案：

1 Do Ethan's friends like his biscuits? (Yes, they do.)

2 Do you like eating or making biscuits? (I like both./I like eating biscuits.)

Let's think

1 Recall the story and match.

2 Circle and say the activities that are in the wrong place.

Outdoor activities

Indoor activities

玩电脑

踢足球

New words

1 Learn the new words.

延伸活动：
学生用新学词汇描述图中人物。如：艾文打球。浩浩不喜欢玩
电脑，他喜欢踢足球。玲玲玩玩具。爱莎看电视，她很高兴。

活动

打球

足球

踢

玩具

玩

电视

高兴

电脑

还是

2 Write the letters and colour the pictures.

a 打球　　b 看电视　　c 踢足球

听听说说 Listen and say

03 **1** Listen and circle the correct answers.

04 **2** Look at the pictures. Listen to the sto

1 男孩喜欢做什么？

第一题录音稿：
1 女孩：回家后，你喜欢打球，还是喜欢玩电脑？
男孩：我喜欢打球。

ⓐ 打球

b 看书

c 玩电脑

2 他们明天做什么？

2 男孩：明天做什么？踢足球怎么样？
女孩：我不喜欢踢足球。我们明天去动物园看老虎。

a 喝茶

b 回家

ⓒ 看老虎

3 他们都喜欢什么活动？

3 男孩：我喜欢踢足球、打球、唱歌。
女孩：我喜欢看电视、打球、玩电脑。

a 看书

ⓑ 打球

c 玩玩具

二题参考问题和答案：
What is Ivan going to do? (He is going to play basketball.)
What is Ethan going to do? (He is going to make biscuits.)
Do you like playing ball games? Answer in Chinese.
(我喜欢/不喜欢打球。)

d say.

3 Look at the pictures. Talk about them with your friend.

她喜欢打球，还是喜欢玩电脑？

打球！

他喜欢踢足球，还是喜欢玩玩具？

他喜欢玩玩具。

Task

Talk about after-school activities with your friend.

参考回答：
我喜欢看书。
我今天回家看书和打球。
我和哥哥一起玩。

你喜欢什么活动？

你今天回家做什么？

你和谁一起玩？

我喜欢……

我今天回家……

我和……一起玩。

Game

提醒学生注意每句话中的关键字，做题时可以从问句或答句着手。如：从答句着手时，答句中的第一句话"这是伊森。"的关键词是"伊森"，而问句a"这是谁？"的"谁"是针对人的疑问词，所以可以确定这两句话是同一组。

Shoot the basketballs to see what Hao Hao is writing about his friend. Write the correct letters in the circles.

a 这是谁？

b 他会不会说英语？

c 他和我是好朋友吗？

d 他喜欢什么活动？

e 他在哪里？

f 他比浩浩高吗？

(a) 这是伊森。

(e) 他在家里。

(f) 他比我高。

(d) 他喜欢做饼干。

(b) 他会说英语。

(c) 我们是好朋友。

Song

🎧 **Listen and sing.**
05

学生一边唱歌，一边配合歌词指认图上的活动。

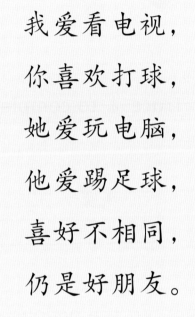

我爱看电视，

你喜欢打球，

她爱玩电脑，

他爱踢足球，

喜好不相同，

仍是好朋友。

延伸活动：

学生熟悉歌曲后，可自编新词，将前四句歌词中的活动替换为其他活动，再唱出来。参考活动：玩玩具、唱歌、画画、做蛋糕、说汉语。

课堂用语 Classroom language

...... +1 ......

你好

....

你可以重复吗？

Can you repeat?

写一写 Write

1 Review and trace the stroke. 老师示范笔画动作，学生跟着做：用手在空中画出"提"。

提

  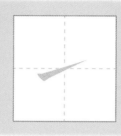 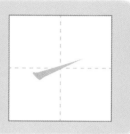

2 Learn the component. Trace 扌 to complete the characters.

学生观察图片，引导他们发现提手旁字与手有关。

3 Look at the pictures. Act out the actions. Colour 扌 in the characters red.

让学生通过用手拥抱、拍打、拉扯和指挥加深对提手旁的理解。做完动作后问问他们这些动作的共同点是什么。

拥抱
to hug

拍打
to clap

拉扯
to pull

指挥
to conduct

4 Trace and write the character.

一 丁 扌 扌 打

打 打

一 二 干 王 王 玎 玎 玗 球
球 球

球 球

5 Write and say.

放学后，我们喜欢
一起 打 球。

汉字小常识 **Did you know?**

Colour the bottom-left component red.

Some characters include a component that is placed on the left and the bottom part of a character.

还

起

翅

迷

这

提醒学生注意这种结构的汉字的书写顺序分两种。一种是先写内部被包围部分，再写包围部分，如"还""迷"和"这"。另一种是先写外部包围部分，再写被包围部分，如"起"和"翅"。

多元学习 Connections

Cultures

20世纪初，乒乓球运动在中国兴起，发展至今已成为国球，但其实它起源于英国，而"乒乓球"这个词则是从英文 ping-pong 音译而来。中国象棋和太极拳都是中国的非物质文化遗产。毽子是中国传统的民俗体育活动，至今已有两千多年历史。

1 Learn about some traditional Chinese activities.

Players hit a lightweight ball back and forth across a table.

Ping-pong

Players play as two armies in a battle to capture the enemy's general.

Chinese chess

T'ai-chi

People practise T'ai-chi, one type of martial arts for defense and health benefits.

Players keep a shuttlecock in the air using their bodies. No hands are allowed!

Jianzi

2 Say the words and ask your friend to do the actions.

打　　踢　　看　　画　　写

Project

1 Find out what activities your classmates like. Write the numbers.

你喜欢打球，还是喜欢玩电脑？

我喜欢打球，不喜欢玩电脑。

多少人喜欢？

打球	
唱歌	
玩玩具	
做饼干	
看电视	
玩电脑	
踢足球	

2 How often do you do the activities in a week? Write the numbers in the pyramid. Do you live a healthy life?

金字塔每一层代表一类活动。第一层是走楼梯、上学走路、骑单车等日常活动，第二层是体育活动，第三层是文娱休闲活动，最上层是看电视、电脑等活动。学生根据自身实际情况进行统计。

你喜欢的活动在上面，还是在下面？

The Activity Pyramid

Cut down on

Twice a week

3-5 times a week

Every-day

学生统计完后与金字塔上的提示进行对比，看看自己的生活习惯是否健康。提醒他们每周要进行适量的体育活动，而最上层的活动应控制时间，以避免久坐和用眼过度。

温习 Checkpoint

老师课前准备几个毽子，可在课上或者课间让学生尝试踢毽子。

1 Complete the questions and learn to play with the shuttlecock.

Say 'I am very happy.' in Chinese. 我很高兴。

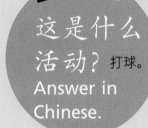
这是什么活动？打球。Answer in Chinese.

这是什么？Answer in Chinese. 这是电脑。

Say 'How about we play with toys?' in Chinese. 我们玩玩具吗？

我们去踢足球，还是去玩玩具？

Say 'Do you like singing or painting?' in Chinese. 你喜欢唱歌，还是画画？

Complete the word.
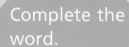
打 球

你喜欢看书，还是看电视？

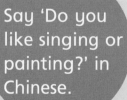

2 Work with your friend. Colour the stars and the chillies.

Words	说	读	写
玩	☆	☆	🌶
活动	☆	☆	🌶
电视	☆	☆	🌶
踢	☆	☆	🌶
足球	☆	☆	🌶
打球	☆	☆	🌶
还是	☆	☆	🌶
玩具	☆	🌶	🌶
电脑	☆	🌶	🌶
高兴	☆	🌶	🌶

Words and sentences	说	读	写
你喜欢玩玩具，还是喜欢看电视？	☆	🌶	🌶
你喜欢吃饼干，还是喜欢做饼干呢？	☆	🌶	🌶

Talk about activities that one likes	☆

3 What does your teacher say?

My teacher says ...

分享 Sharing

延伸活动：
1 学生用手遮盖英文，读中文单词，并思考单词意思
2 学生用手遮盖中文单词，看着英文说出对应的中文单
3 学生两人一组，尽量运用中文单词分角色复述故事

Words I remember

玩	wán	to play
活动	huó dòng	activity
电视	diàn shì	television
踢	tī	to kick
足球	zú qiú	football
打球	dǎ qiú	to play ball games
还是	hái shì	or
玩具	wán jù	toy
电脑	diàn nǎo	computer
高兴	gāo xìng	happy

Other words

放学	fàng xué	school is over
回家	huí jiā	to go home
后	hòu	after, afterwards
很多	hěn duō	many
觉得	jué dé	think of
怎么样	zěn me yàng	how
分享	fēn xiǎng	to share

OXFORD
UNIVERSITY PRESS

Oxford University Press is a department of the University of Oxford.
It furthers the University's objective of excellence in research, scholarship,
and education by publishing worldwide. Oxford is a registered trade mark of
Oxford University Press in the UK and in certain other countries

Published in Hong Kong by
Oxford University Press (China) Limited
39th Floor, One Kowloon, 1 Wang Yuen Street, Kowloon Bay,
Hong Kong

© Oxford University Press (China) Limited 2017

Illustrated by Anne Lee, KK Ng, KY Chan and Wildman

Photographs for reproduction permitted by Dreamstime.com

China National Publications Import & Export (Group) Corporation is an authorized distributor of
Oxford Elementary Chinese.

Please contact content@cnpiec.com.cn or 86-10-65856782

ISBN: 978-0-19-082201-9

10 9 8 7 6 5 4 3 2

Teacher's Edition
ISBN: 978-0-19-082213-2

10 9 8 7 6 5 4 3 2